The Invisible Made Visible

C.W. Lewis

To DAVE
FROM
C W Lewis

Published in 2007 by C.W. Lewis

Copyright © C.W. Lewis 2005

All rights reserved. No part of this publication may be reproduced, stored in a retrieval system, or transmitted by any means, electronic, mechanical, photocopying or otherwise, without the prior permission of the publisher.

ISBN: 978-0-9556050-0-0

Typeset and Printed in Great Britain by
CPI Antony Rowe
Bumpers Farm, Chippenham, Wiltshire

CONTENTS

	INTRODUCTION	1
1	REVEALING THE TRUTH	3
2	A PLACE CALLED HEAVEN	9
3	CREATION OF A TEMPORARY LIFE ON EARTH	15
4	EVOLUTION OF MAN	19
5	CHOSEN PEOPLE	25
6	THE COMING OF GODS REPRESENTATIVE	31
7	THE FALSE PROPHET	41
8	END OF ALL LIFE ON EARTH	45
9	UNDERSTANDING HEAVENLY KNOWLEDGE	49
10	A ONENESS IN ALL	63
11	WHY WE ALL NEED THE COMFORTER	73

INTRODUCTION

This book that is written through me is the key to the door of the vessel which is heavenly, because now in studying this heavenly knowledge in this book you are reading heavenly knowledge from God, which will open the vessel which is heavenly because you are guaranteed you are reading heavenly knowledge from God. If you want to enter you need this knowledge, which is the key to open up the heavenly vessel so you can grow to a heavenly being within that vessel.

This vessel is in the brain that all beings in this world have male or female that has been closed because only one vessel was needed and one character was needed.

As God promised in the end times he would send a comforter for us. God now has put knowledge in this world through me so that this vessel which is heavenly that we have in the brain in all beings male or female, can now be opened with this knowledge that I have written in this book. In you studying this knowledge which is the key to opening up this vessel, so knowledge that comes from this vessel that is in books can enter into this vessel that this scripture has now opened and the knowledge that enters in which is heavenly that came from this vessel will now grow in this vessel to create a heavenly character.

The brain was made for this purpose of creating a fleshly character from the fleshly vessel it has and in the end times now through this vessel which is heavenly which was closed but now can be opened it can create through the heavenly knowledge filling this vessel a heavenly being within. So if you as a fleshly being now because you are in the end times want to create a heavenly being within you will have to study this knowledge in this book given to me by God for all beings in the world male or female. This knowledge which God promised in the end times to comfort us is the promised knowledge that he said would come and through this knowledge he will open this closed vessel because this scripture is the only knowledge that can open this closed vessel. So that this vessel when opened can receive heavenly knowledge to create a heavenly being and a likeness of a heavenly being. You as a being are comforted by walking in this world with a fleshly character, which you are and a heavenly character which you are now.

Therefore God's promise has been fulfilled in that the comforter is within you until the end.

Chapter 1

REVEALING THE TRUTH

There is only one knowledge that is true. I have received this knowledge by God opening up my heavenly vessel. I have had opened up the part of the brain that is not used for everyday thinking but when opened can receive the true knowledge, so I as a body, with a brain, like everyone else, have had opened up a part of the brain that can receive this knowledge. With this part of the brain, I know the truth and it is the truth I want to write in this book, as a messenger so that everyone who reads this book will know the truth as it is revealed to me. This book will be about knowledge I receive in the part of my brain not known by everyday thinking.

This book explains our life on earth, why our life is made this way and what happens to us and the world. It also explains our purpose on this earth, where we go at the end of the world and why it has to be.

I have only been able to write this book with heavenly knowledge revealed to me and I could not have written it without it.

The knowledge I receive to enable me to write this book comes to me from a vessel which has been opened up and fills itself drawing in knowledge which is heavenly. This knowledge is there for anyone who reads the scripture which I have been guided to write which will open up your vessel to receive heavenly knowledge showing us that knowing fleshly knowledge is not the same as knowing heavenly knowledge. Heavenly knowledge is heavenly knowledge and fleshly knowledge is fleshly knowledge.

We have a vessel which guides us by filling itself with fleshly knowledge, which makes us walk in this world as a fleshly character. We also have a vessel which can be filled with heavenly knowledge to guide you to knowing you are a heavenly character.

When you are guided by fleshly knowledge from that fleshly vessel you walk as a character with fleshly knowledge, feeding the brain and guiding you to a character for fleshly things. When you draw from that vessel filled with heavenly knowledge you draw in knowledge, which is heavenly. This heavenly knowledge feeds the brain so that you understand and know heavenly things. This heavenly knowledge guides you to growing a heavenly being within.

When this vessel filled with heavenly knowledge feeds your brain to understand heavenly thoughts and knowledge your brain is shut off from fleshly thoughts and knowledge. Then the brain, which guides the body becomes a son, brother and a saint because heavenly knowledge feeding the brain tells you this. Only when you are in that heavenly vessel guided by heavenly knowledge are you a son, brother and a saint. It is not a fleshly son, brother and saint you are but only in the eyes of God.

Whether you are male or female if you have found that heavenly vessel drawing in knowledge to feed you, to knowing heavenly things then that knowledge will tell you and give you an understanding and reassurance that you are a son, brother and a saint. Being one knowledge and understanding, which all heavenly vessels are filled with makes you one in the eyes of God. This is because of the heavenly knowledge he has put in this world to fill any heavenly vessel, which has been opened. Any being who has worked hard to get to know and find this knowledge to make him or her a oneness with God with the thoughts and knowledge reassuring them makes them one with God. In that oneness when you are guided by this knowledge you are as one knowing you are a son, brother and a saint in the eyes of God. When that vessel is shut and you are guided by fleshly knowledge you are just a fleshly character walking this world seen and known in a fleshly way. It is only when the heavenly vessel is opened and feeding your brain with heavenly knowledge are you that heavenly being.

It is only heavenly knowledge guiding you while you are in that vessel to know heavenly knowledge so you as a being can understand it. It is not to guide you to do heavenly things only to know heavenly things.

I am guided to write this heavenly knowledge so we as beings can understand the purpose of why God had to make the world as it is and why we are for that purpose only. I have to write why life is only for the place we are in now so we can understand our purpose and life as it was meant to be and is told to me.

No one in this world was made for a heavenly life only for a fleshly life. Guided by this heavenly knowledge I will give you understanding of our purpose and future so you can be assured that what I have written through this knowledge is the truth. You can see our lives unfold in a way that we do not understand because fleshly thoughts and knowledge only guide us to know life on earth as fleshly. Fleshly thoughts guide us to fleshly ways and understanding and beliefs and to follow rituals of a different way of life. We as fleshly beings see our way as right because of the way we see our lives and because of fleshly thoughts guiding people to different knowledge. Fleshly thoughts guide beings to a life confusing what is right and wrong because we see our way of thinking and our way of life as right. We see other ways of life as wrong. Fleshly thoughts guide beings to confuse what is right or wrong. Different rights and wrongs are seen as right by some followings but seen as wrong by other followings.

Therefore fleshly knowledge causes confusion on what is right or wrong.

This knowledge which is heavenly and which is only one knowledge and can only have one understanding has come to make a oneness. This is so we as fleshly beings will know our purpose of life and our future. A oneness with this knowledge could be made so that this confusion we have with knowledge that is fleshly will be made right by the knowledge which is heavenly.

An understanding will be there for all people of the world so that there will be no confusion anymore. This knowledge is only one understanding and one way. This heavenly knowledge is forthcoming because now is the time that we as beings with a confused mind can have real understanding of our purpose and future.

CHAPTER 2

A PLACE CALLED HEAVEN

"Heaven is where the expanding light is in the universe. If you can see the expanding light in the universe that is where Heaven is".

Heaven is a physical place. Not a physical place as on earth, but a physical place where things are made permanent. All life created in Heaven is permanent. Heaven is permanent and life on earth is temporary.

Heaven has not always been physical. Heaven was made physical by the expanding physical, which entered the place of the invisible.

The invisible was building blocks of life, which had not yet got together to create a life. Although there was life it was not as we know it. It was only with the getting together of the building blocks which were invisible that visible life was created. When the expanding physical entered the invisible pushing the building blocks together they became a physical life.

The first creation made visible entered the place of the visible. Seeing itself as visible and

seeing more invisible being made visible entering the visible, the first creation looked at the visible and decided an order would have to be made. This was so the presence of visible would be seen as compatible and pleasant to the eye. An order would be needed because there was now a visible life in the place of the visible. The first creation created an understanding in itself which would give a fair judgement of a life that could be lived in a visible way so all visible would enjoy the life of the visible. An order could be maintained in what could be created as pleasurable to the eye, so a beautiful place and a happy contented place could be achieved. Shapes and sizes were approved by the first visibles' understanding. An order could be maintained in that all shapes and sizes would be pleasurable to the eye and fit in with the life, which was to come.

As life progressed and a communication was approved by the understanding, names were given so they were recognisable. The first invisible with the understanding was named God, so he would be recognised as the first visible.

Heaven grew into a beautiful place with guidance of the first visibles' understanding. That is how Heaven was made in this way. All visible which was made could create its own pleasures and create things which were pleasurable. The name Heaven became known because of the beauty and tranquillity, which came with these creations, which were made. Heavenly life expanded so that life in Heaven became plentiful and pleasurable and a certain way of life was established which made all life a oneness. This life would go on forever and never die because the building blocks of life which life was made of had building blocks of life within which renewed all life and creation. This meant life and creation would never die.

Life in Heaven carried on living this way until the light of the universe which was expanding came to the edge of the expanding visible where the Heavenly place was. The invading bright light invaded the Heavenly place making it very bright.

Life in the Heavenly place seeing the brightness gradually cover their Heavenly place took advantage of the brightness in creating a life different from the life they already had. They made the Heavenly place a divided place so Heaven had in its place a new way of life. God approved of this way of life and saw that they were happy and contented living this new way of life. He saw that Heaven was divided by the two ways of life caused by the brightness of the invading light. God saw the contentment and happiness of both ways of life, the old way of life being happy and contented and the new way of life being happy and contented. The oneness was in the happy and contented lives he approved of.

The life in Heaven lived a happy life until some of the Heavenly beings went to God asking him if he would ask all Heavenly beings living the old way to come and live the new way. God told these beings of the new way who wanted this that this could not be done. This is because he approved of both ways of life, which were happy and contented and the oneness that was in the happy and contented lives of the two ways of life.

The Heavenly beings went back to the beings living the new way and told them that God would not give them the requests they asked for, so they agreed that they would go back to God and ask him to consider the requests they asked him to do. God being approached by these beings living the new way knew they really wanted him to do the things they asked of him. Seeing they only wanted him to make Heaven one with the two ways of life being made one again God told them it could not be done. This was because of the confusion it would cause in trying to bring one way of life to live another way of life. God told them the two happy and contented ways of life were the oneness.

God seeing their disapproval at what he had said told them he would show them two ways of life trying to be made one and the confusion it would cause. He would not show them the two ways of life being made one in a Heavenly place but he would show them two ways trying to be made one in a different place. This was so they could witness what could happen to the two ways of life approved by him trying to be made one way of life. God made a plan so that two ways of life could be made by him as an example representing two ways of life in a Heavenly place. A place had to be found where this could take place.

Chapter 3

CREATION OF TEMPORARY LIFE ON EARTH

God needed a place where temporary life could be made, he decided earth was ideal and would be a suitable living place. God who is a creator of permanent life in a heavenly place had to create a temporary life on earth.

God's plan was to create two halves so each half joining together would create its own life and likeness. God's plan was to create a life who could go on to create its own life so he would not be needed after in the temporary world. This meant the two halves he created could be taken back, leaving the lives the two halves had created to carry on creating their own lives in their own likeness which would be temporary. This meant temporary lives of this nature could live a long life by each temporary life creating another temporary life which together would create one long life. All creation would be made this way with temporary life joining together to create a long life.

Before this creation of life could be created God had to create food for his creation to survive on. He had to make the earth fertile so that food would grow and be plentiful for all species to live on. He waited for the right time until he saw it was ready.

Seeds were planted so that when they grew they would give off seeds so that they would have a temporary life joining together, so food would be made plentiful. All food made this way came from seeds growing and creating other seeds so God could withdraw the first seeds. All life and all seeds would rely on their own creation, all life was made this way.

The food became plentiful then small insects and smaller animals were made. This was so the food being eaten by the small animals and insects would spread seeds further apart and fertilize the land by the food they ate. As the land became more fertile God planted more seeds of different varieties and trees of different varieties. This was so the land that was barren would become fertile and habitable for every species of life that would be coming to earth. These fertile places grew in size so then bigger animals were introduced to eat more food and fertilize the land in a bigger way. God saw what he was doing looked good and introduced much bigger animals and birds so that the fertile land could spread all around the world by them eating vast amounts of food. This food was transferred to other parts making it fertile until the world was a fertile place.

When the world was a fertile place then life could be introduced of a different nature. God saw it was time for his beings to be introduced to this world which was the purpose of him making the world a liveable place.

God introduced human beings into this world because the time was right for them to be here. He planted an egg containing two halves of one life and another egg containing two halves of another life. So one egg produced with its two halves a man and the other egg with its two halves produced a woman. One life needed the other life so that a temporary life could be made this way. The joining together of the one life with the other life created one life.

All life was made this way in human beings, animals and every creature that walked in this world, all relying on two lives coming together to create one life. Some were created male and some were created female.

Life created from a heavenly place created a life to create its own life which was temporary. The first lives created which were two halves could be taken back to a heavenly place so that after all life in this world created its own life.

All life having the will to live survived pursuing short lives which were temporary reproducing temporary lives joining together to make and create long life.

Now the plan he had for man and woman from the beginning of their creation to the end of the world can start.

Chapter 4

EVOLUTION OF MAN

When God made human beings ready to walk in this world he gave them a brain and a mind. This guided them with knowledge so they could gradually build a life of their own in this world. The brain was big so it could take a being of this nature from the beginning of life walking in this world right through to the end of life in this world. The thinking of the mind was a gradual process with the mind receiving knowledge slowly, which over the years altered the lives of these beings. Although the process was gradual human beings altered as the process gained more knowledge and it made them more aware of the life that they were capable of living. Life is invisible in that knowledge gathered is invisible and will be made visible by the things we do.

The human brain is the most important and sacred thing in the world. That is why it is essential that we as beings will survive the duration of the life of the brain. Evolution is the progress of the brain. It is not what we want to do with it, it is what it wants to do with us. The brain is the most important thing to be passed on, including the memory, so the body has to be renewed for the brain to survive.

When God created man his brain was different from a woman's brain. He made man first and woman second. Both were important in the creation of life on earth in order to create another being. The man supplies the brain for the new body and the woman supplies the body for the brain.

When human beings started out their brain was like a child which did not contain any knowledge. When the brain first formed it was fresh. It is used more now so it is wearing out and cannot cope with the demands it puts on itself. It is not the body wearing out because that keeps renewing itself, but the brains of today create a brain for tomorrow. When a brain of today creates a brain of tomorrow in a babies body the baby is born with a new brain of a child. The brain of the child will have to cope with more things because of the progress of the brain before it. As the brain creates new things and ideas and a new brain is born that brain has to take in more knowledge and is used more. It is the brain reaching its fulfilment. We have been guardians of the brain from the day when the brain was a child to the brain being an adult. The life which was first is still here to the end.

When an old brain dies leaving its knowledge in the world the things the old brain has achieved is remembered by newer brains being born. When a new brain is born it takes in all knowledge of the world and any new knowledge in its lifetime is also passed on.

We have evolved from a child brain to an adult brain, which has taken a lifetime on the earth to evolve. From one child to one man the first brain will become the last because men and women of yesterday grew into men and women of today. This is an evolution of the brain, which needed a long gradual expansion to get to its full capacity because everything in this world is temporary. The brain has to keep being renewed to reach a stage it was made for.

The brain is coming to the stage when it will be filled to capacity and no more knowledge will be able to be received. All beings are inspired by knowledge, which they draw on to guide them. The world is full now of beings with a mind that is nearly filled with things they know and can do. Knowledge is gathered by the brain and alters what the body is capable of achieving by collecting new knowledge when doing new things. Therefore the gradual progress of the body reacts with the progress of the brain. Knowledge filling the brain to do more things and discover more makes the body do more things and the body react accordingly. The purpose of man being created as a body, which is flexible is being able to bend to the desires and demands of the brain as it progresses so when the brain is progressing the body will bend accordingly. The body is the protector of the brain. It is the brain that guides the body to do the things it does.

The brain is the most important thing, but we see the body as important and we make it look attractive to other bodies in a physical way. The unseen brain and what it can achieve is hidden so it is the physical side of the body that is attractive and gives the urge to carry on reproducing. The responsibility of the brain is passed on to other bodies through reproducing so the brain can evolve. We as modern beings of today owe our way of life to bodies and minds of the past, so what they went through starting as a baby mind in an adult body have progressed to our stature and looks today. Bodies are only temporary and have to be renewed by producing other bodies.

For the brain to develop and carry on progressing, new bodies are guided to fill their brain with new knowledge and understanding. All knowledge and memory is passed on from generation to generation. This means the life of the brain can survive in this world right to the end. We are temporary on this earth and no one can live forever. Advancement of the brain will live for the duration of life on earth.

The mind guiding the body alters the body to the environment it is in and the tasks required. So as we are guided through life from beginning to end the body, which was made flexible alters to the task that the mind gives it.

In the beginning the body stayed the same for long periods because the mind was not using it in a way to alter it. As the mind developed and tasks were required by the body, the body altered gradually in posture, looks and size according to tasks required. If lifting or heavy work was required of the body because the mind guided it, muscles and strength were needed so the body could do the tasks required of it.

The body altered accordingly to what tasks the brain guided it to do. Muscles can be built through devices we have made and this applies to both men and women. The food we have developed can alter the body and appearance because the products we now eat can change our growth and size so that we can be big people or small people. The brain is developed more by us wanting more and doing more so the brain has to take all this in and develop to its maximum in what it can do in the body it is in. The body at the beginning looked different than it does now because of the gradual process of the brain receiving knowledge guiding the body to do small things. A brain of little knowledge at the beginning did and achieved small chores. The brain of today receives more knowledge to think more and do more. It has adapted the body to this way of life. The brain is a creative brain but it creates physical things not living things. So physical things are made to represent living things so they can move accordingly to our needs.

We as beings have done a brilliant job bringing the brain through this world protecting it and passing it on to this day, so that it is a creator of life and showing its capabilities. The brain which was first is still here at the end.

Now it is time for the brain to tell us its purpose and its destination. It has been a long slow process altering the thinking of the brain to guide the body to do things by altering its stature and abilities.

God has filled and nearly completed his plan for what the earth and beings were made for.

Chapter 5

CHOSEN PEOPLE

All human life made for this world was here to create a life on the earth. This was so that when the time was right God could put his beings in this world to create a life suitable to represent a heavenly life.

God seeing it was time to put his plan into action planted an egg into the ground. Two bodies would come from this one egg, one male and one female. The male would be first and the female second both from the same egg.

The brain of these two bodies, one male and one female would be different from beings created before them. Both these bodies one male and one female had a brain each and each brain had two vessels. One vessel for heavenly knowledge and one vessel for fleshly knowledge. This meant these two bodies could walk in the world with two vessels instead of beings before who could only use one of their vessels which was the fleshly one.

The beings before with one vessel could only receive fleshly knowledge, but the two beings God made could walk in this world with two vessels, one for fleshly knowledge and one for heavenly knowledge. They would have a choice of which vessel they would like to influence the brain to a life that they saw would be good for them. God let them walk into a beautiful place where they could choose whether to draw on fleshly knowledge or heavenly knowledge to live their life. They could only have one life either fleshly or heavenly.

God left them alone to choose and when he came to visit them he saw they had chosen the fleshly way. God was very sad because he wanted beings in this world that would represent heavenly beings, but now he only had fleshly beings guided by fleshly knowledge. God allowed them to live in this world as fleshly beings but shut up the vessel that would have guided them to living and representing heavenly beings. This meant when they got together and produced other bodies they would only produce bodies with a brain and mind influencing the brain to a life of fleshly knowledge.

God hoping a good life would come from the life he had planted in this world even though it was not guided by heavenly knowledge, told them to go forth and multiply. This was so that he could see the life that would come from them because they chose a fleshly way of life to represent a heavenly life.

God seeing the life in this world progressing and multiplying still had hope that a good life could be made to represent his heavenly life. God allowed all life to progress, waiting for a time when he could choose a life that would be suitable to represent heavenly beings and a heavenly life on the earth.

As time went by and different generations went and new generations were born, God could see that life in this world was not right to represent heavenly life in this world. Then the time came when God saw there was a people trying to go the right way but they were hindered by the place they lived and the things they saw and the influences around them. God thought of a way to save this small group of people trying to live a good life and he made a plan.

God spoke to a senior person of this group and told him what would happen. This senior person was bewildered at first at the message he received from God but went along with this message and was ready for the plan that God had for them.

This plan was to free this group from the influences and the life that surrounded them so they could live their good way and not be influenced by seeing things which could make them go astray. God destroyed the influences that surrounded them and cleansed the earth where they lived so they would not be influenced by the things that surrounded them. This meant they could live alone producing more life from that good life. God hoped this could be the life that could represent his heavenly life on the earth.

God saw what he did was not good but it was needed so that a good life could be made for the purpose that we as beings were put here for.

God saw the life they had was progressing well so he left them alone so they could get on with the tasks ahead of them. He cleared the path so no distractions were close to influence them.

As they multiplied and new generations were born and passed God noticed that some had spread and were being influenced by other ways of life. God seeing this had to change his plan and was sad at the choice he had to make. He spoke to a senior person who had responsibility and who people listened to and gave him strict rules, which they were to live by. It was fear of God showing him these demands that brought him to the people, telling them and showing them the demands God had given them to carry out.

God assisted this man to lead the people of

that nation to the way of life he set out for them to live. God now had a people that would represent the heavenly beings on the earth.

As life progressed God saw this nation were doing their best to live the way he guided them to live and that they would pass on the knowledge. When the first person who had this knowledge which was written down died, the knowledge which was written down was passed on to future minds so this knowledge would never be forgotten.

God allowed this written word of God to be written so that this nation would be the chosen people and have God on their side. They would know through this written word of God and the knowledge that was written down that they were special people chosen by God and loved by God for the task that was ahead of them.

As the nation grew God came to more leaders of this nation assuring them and guiding them making them a strong nation. The written word of God had Gods knowledge guiding people to do the things God wanted them to do. He also guided them to make a pledge with him that they would represent Gods people on earth. God saw that they were strong in what they believed. All people around knew they were different in the way they acted and the things they did.

To celebrate that they were the chosen ones the written word of God was written to tell anyone who read it that these people of this nation were the chosen people of God. God watched his nation of people growing and saw that they would sacrifice their lives to keep this written word of God alive from generation to generation. The writing and meaning was more than life itself to them.

God saw his nation he had chosen and the people of this nation were now ready for God to put his own representative in this world to represent himself. This being that he would make in this world would be born in that nation that he had chosen to represent himself.

They would know that they were living the way God wanted them to live by their courage and conviction in sticking to Gods knowledge, that was in the written word of God which meant more to them than their own lives.

Chapter 6

THE COMING OF GODS REPRESENTATIVE

God saw it was time for him to be represented in this world, so he had to create a being in this world for this purpose. God created an egg, which would grow to represent him. The egg he created would grow a body with a mind and a brain, which he could guide to represent himself.

God chose in this world a woman who would bear that baby who would grow to represent himself. God chose a woman who was fresh and capable of looking after this child. He also chose a man to look after the woman and the child, this meant the child would have a mother and a father to take responsibility for bringing up that child. God planted the egg in the woman he chose to be right for this purpose so the egg would be seen as her own egg reproducing this baby.

Before the baby was born the man and the woman knew the baby was not theirs, because of heavenly knowledge telling them so, but they still took on the responsibility of having it seen as their own. This is so that the baby would be seen to be born normal as expected in the way of this world.

Heavenly knowledge from heavenly beings guided the woman who was to bear the baby. When the baby was to be born the knowledge of the heavenly beings would influence the parents of this baby to make sure it was well looked after. The parents knew the baby would be special because of the influence of the heavenly beings putting understanding in their minds. This made them feel good and confident and proud to be looking after and taking the responsibility of such a special child. The baby was to be born into this world as a mind and a brain and a body that would be influenced by God to a heavenly understanding.

The presence of the heavenly beings caused a brightness in the sky. Their presence was to influence some minds in this world to an understanding of the importance of this baby who was to be born. They also influenced the chosen parents to guide them to a safe place where the baby would be born.

The knowledge and understanding from these heavenly beings went out to the highest people in the land. This brought forth kings to the place where the king of all kings was born.

The kings could witness a king who was born above all kings. When the kings saw the baby that was born, their minds influenced by knowledge from heavenly beings who were looking after the baby knew they had witnessed a king above all kings come into this world. The kings gave homage to the baby knowing he would be a greater king than themselves.

When the parents saw that the kings were paying homage to their child they knew this child was special. This special child who was born into the world was not of the making of the parents. They were only assigned to bear and look after his child. This was only so that the baby would be born as normal and recognised as a normal birth with normal parents. The parents took the child and were guided by heavenly knowledge so they would be guided to a safe place in order to look after the child and act accordingly.

As the child grew and did all the same things as other children he was seen as no different from other children. As the child grew older and grew in stature and abilities he became more knowledgeable about the traditions and keepings of the word that was in the writings from prophets. These writings were guided by God and were used to build a nation of people to represent heavenly life on the earth. This nation of people walked as Gods chosen people through the writings they read, the traditions that they obeyed and with laws that were needed for them to be seen as the chosen people. God chose for his child to be brought up in the presence of these chosen people.

This special boy grew into a learned scholar in heavenly knowledge, he made other scholars look at him in a way where they were surprised at the knowledge he knew even though he was a young boy. As time passed he did things that were expected of him and he was recognised as just an ordinary being with skills and knowledge in the place where he lived. As he grew and gained more knowledge and did more things God could see the being he made was coming to an end of a time just being an ordinary being and being recognised as just ordinary. It was time for his life to be changed. God guided this being to a place where he would be recognised as the being he was to be and was made for.

He was recognised as the being he was to be by the being that had knowledge that gave him recognition of who this being was. He was guided by the knowledge of God to a place where he could be changed from the being he was recognised as, as a fleshly being to a being of a different nature and guidance. This was so he could be a being representing God in this world and God could guide this being in a different way.

His guidance of fleshly knowledge making him a fleshly being was shut up and a new vessel was opened which would guide him in a heavenly way. This was so he could walk on earth representing a Godly being so that God had a representative of himself. He could guide that being in this world to do special things and be recognised as someone special by the things he was guided and able to do. The words he was guided to say would make him a heavenly representative of God.

God through his being he made would guide beings to a life representing a new heavenly way of life different from the heavenly way of life he guided beings before to represent. This was so there would be a new people representing heavenly life in a different way than ones before him.

When this being came down from where he had been changed he was welcomed by other beings that were assigned to follow him and be guided by him. They recognised that they were the first beings of this new life that was to come as they walked in this world. This being was guided by Gods knowledge to do things that had never been seen on the earth before and speaking words and knowledge that had never been heard before. He had more power in the things he could do and the words he spoke in that his words were above all words spoken in this world and his knowledge was above all knowledge in this world. The things he did were above all things that could be done in this world.

People who heard his words and admired his knowledge could not believe what they saw and what he had done and achieved. When he presented himself in different places he left a presence everywhere he went because they knew he was different and special. They were joyous there was someone like this in this world walking amongst them.

People started to turn to him for his words and knowledge and the things he could do and achieve. He brought joyous things to the people in what he had achieved and showed them. All the people that saw him and followed him were recognising and knowing him as someone special. God was pleased with the being he had made to represent him and the being was happy at the way he was guided by Gods heavenly knowledge doing the things he could making people of this world happy.

The things he did and the knowledge he had and the words he spoke were challenged by people who could not recognise the being he was. This was because of the teachings they had through God before him. They could not recognise him as a being of God doing and saying these things. They doubted him because they were guided to represent a different way of life. He was going up against their knowledge and the writings they had from Gods heavenly place. This was to guide them to represent heavenly beings, which made them special in that they were the chosen people for these tasks put before them.

The being representing God still carried on saying these words guided by God so the people who followed him were changing and were accepting he was someone special. As time went by and his words and knowledge and the things he did progressed he spread out gathering in more people. These people were waiting for his visits so they could see the things he did and hear the words he spoke. Therefore he became a well known figure in that land so people came from far away to see this being who was different.

When God saw his representative on earth had finished the work that was required of him through his guidance he guided him to a place where he would be changed to a being of the flesh again. All the things that would happen to him would be to the fleshly being he was, not the being representing himself. It would not be the being that he was that would be set upon it would be a fleshly being that would be set upon.

God shut up the vessel, which he had guided his being to do heavenly things with and opened up the vessel to guide him to do fleshly things.

They came to set upon him in that they were to destroy him because of the things he did which they could not understand. They took him to be judged on the things he had done so that their knowledge and life would be seen as righteous. When this being was taken to be judged and he was judged to be unrighteous, he was killed in a way where he was seen by all to have been killed. God allowed this to happen to this being so that there were witnesses that he had died.

God who made this being from a heavenly creation would take back this being so no trace of him would be in this world.

As customs required they put his body in a tomb that was to be sealed like other bodies would be. God would take this body that had died witnessed by beings, there at the time. He would make this body change into the being that represented him with the mind, which was heavenly. This meant this being could walk in this world for a while showing anyone that saw and recognised him that he was not a normal being because he came back from the dead to walk among them. They would not forget him because he had not died and he would teach them and guide them to do things that were required of them. He would guide them in knowledge and understanding so they could walk as he walked in this world doing and saying things in a similar fashion as he had done. When he was to leave this world they could carry on doing similar things and speaking similar knowledge so they would be seen as different by following in his footsteps.

As time went by it was time for him to leave this world because he was not made to stay just to visit and leave an everlasting presence and knowledge in this world. All those that would follow him in doing these things and saying these words would be looked on as people with authority on heavenly things. God withdrew the being he made from this world representing himself and left them to do the things required of them.

In this world there was a being who was persecuting them so God speaking to this being would change him from being a persecutor. He would change him to a being who would follow the way that would guide him so he would do the same things and speak the same words as the beings who he was persecuting. God guided them all to go out to the nations saying his words and doing the things required of them. They were seen as special by the people that would be witnesses of what they said and did.

As time went by and they were growing older the knowledge they had would have to be remembered in a way so that it would not be forgotten. God guided them through their mind so they could put in writing the life of the being who he made to represent himself. They could also write about their own experiences they saw as witnesses so that what they spoke would be believed.

All the writings had been put down with the beings passing on knowledge that was experienced and the things they did. The words they spoke could be read and understood so that generation after generation would know the things that were done by the being he made representing himself. Generations would know the things he had done and spoken about after he had been taken up to a heavenly place. God had words written down in this world so his representative would never be forgotten.

Chapter 7

THE FALSE PROPHET

God saw that the time was right and the world was ready to receive two beings, a man and a woman so that they could create a life to represent a heavenly way of life. They would be given the choice whether to represent the heavenly way of life on earth with a fleshly mind or to represent a heavenly way of life with a heavenly mind. Because only one mind was needed and they chose the fleshly mind God shut up the mind which was heavenly so that life in this world would only have one mind which is fleshly to represent a heavenly way of life.

In this world we only have one mind guiding us to heavenly things, so we are not to blame for the way of life trying to live in a heavenly way with a fleshly mind. We had no choice we had to follow it this way.

The false prophet is the mind, which is confused. We as fleshly beings with a fleshly mind cannot understand heavenly things. The fleshly mind that knows fleshly things from its fleshly vessel is confused trying to give you understanding of heavenly things when it only knows fleshly things about heavenly things. We have a mind that only understands fleshly things trying to guide us to knowing heavenly things, making us blind in what we see as heavenly things. Therefore in life we are being guided by a mind about heavenly things when it only knows fleshly things.

Now in the last times, knowledge, which is heavenly and a mind, which is heavenly is here to relieve the fleshly mind from its duties of guiding us to heavenly things in a fleshly way. Now in the end times we have a vessel and mind, which is heavenly that can guide us to heavenly things.

Now when we want to know fleshly knowledge the mind which is fleshly only has to supply us with fleshly knowledge. Now when we want to know heavenly knowledge we go to the mind that knows heavenly things. The mind, which is fleshly, can rest when we want to know heavenly things and the heavenly mind can rest when we want to know fleshly things.

The false prophet was the mind, which was fleshly trying to guide us to knowing heavenly things. Being blind in heavenly things now seeing straight because the mind, which was fleshly was relieved from its duty of supplying us with heavenly knowledge. Now healed because now the mind is happy with supplying just fleshly knowledge because now there is a mind to supply us with heavenly knowledge.

Both minds are at peace with themselves because knowledge now is separated into two minds and two vessels. One fleshly mind only knowing fleshly things and one heavenly mind only knowing heavenly things.

We were blind now we can see because the vessel that was shut is now open so heavenly knowledge for the last times can be understood.

We as beings have a knowledge in this world to fill the heavenly vessel to guide us this way, which is the heavenly way. So in our last times in this world we can walk as a fleshly being knowing fleshly things and a heavenly being knowing heavenly things, having two minds guiding the brain in creating two characters, one fleshly and one heavenly. The heavenly character is seen by all beings that have this vessel filled with knowledge which is heavenly, which has only come in the last times to comfort us in us knowing this knowledge which is heavenly guiding the brain through the mind which is heavenly to knowing this heavenly likeness. It is in this state of mind, which is heavenly for when the brain gives up its life in the end times. The vessel filled with fleshly knowledge gives up the knowledge, which is fleshly so the character, which is fleshly, leaves the vessel in a fleshly way. The vessel, which is heavenly filled with heavenly knowledge in the last times, gives the brain an understanding and a likeness in that the comfort the brain has in the last times sees a heavenly likeness and a heavenly knowledge that the brain has in itself in its vessel which is heavenly emptying itself of the knowledge which is heavenly from the vessel which is heavenly and seeing the likeness of the heavenly being and the knowledge of the heavenly being going up to a heavenly place because the likeness is of a heavenly being and the knowledge comes from a heavenly place.

Therefore the part of the brain has a feeling that a part of it has gone to a heavenly place, so the brain is comforted in the last time. As God promised in the end times we would have a comforter to comfort us in a heavenly way.

Chapter 8

END OF ALL LIFE ON EARTH

The end comes when God sees that the life in this world has had its full use and is coming to an end with the purpose of this life at its climax.

In the last days on earth, the brain that has been with us since the beginning of time is being used to its full capacity. The brain that is made by man and woman and put in a body at the end of time is filled quickly, this is because of the chores and tasks we now require it to do. As the brain has been here a long time from beginning to end the brain that is made by man has got weaker because of the time the brain has been in this world. We use the brain that is weaker than when first made to push it to its limits, so the brain itself will give up the will to go on because of the pressure and demands we put on it. The brain is not so strong and fresh now as it was in the beginning when it was hardly used. The brain has grown from a fresh brain with not much knowledge to a brain that has been in this world for a long time being used to its limits.

The brain will give up the will to go on. This will happen to all living things in the end. The will to live and go on will be withdrawn. The purpose we have been put here for would have been fulfilled. All life in the air, sea and on land will give up the will to live because there is no more purpose.

Men, women and children in this world at the end will lay down where they are and the brain will die.

In the dying process in the last days the memory that feeds the brain to a life that creates a character fades away so there is just an emptiness. The emptiness causes the brain to be relieved of the pressure of life that it has achieved and the character that this vessel has gathered to guide the brain to guide the body to a life. Then the life that was achieved to create a character fades away. The empty vessel goes back to emptiness and in that emptiness the brain that was dying feels peace, ecstasy and relief and feels comfortable and there is no more pressure put on it. The food of life gathered to feed the brain to guide the body will disappear. In this process the thoughts and whispers that were gathered in the life of this character will be given up. Then those thoughts and whispers that he or she had while being that character, go out and will be received by the characters that they were aimed at. All whispers and thoughts of the character that you were in this life will be received from other characters who aim their thoughts and whispers at you as a character. In the dying process there is an emptying of the vessel of the character you were in this world. Then the empty vessel gathers in the thoughts and whispers from other characters about the way you as an individual lived your life in this world. You are judged by the way you live your life in this world by the thoughts and whispers about you as a character on people seeing you living your life, not as you see yourself living your life. You are judged by people who have experienced you living your life in this world and how they see you have presented your life. All life is judged, you judging people's lives by your thoughts and them judging your life by their thoughts about you.

When this process is finished and all thoughts and whispers are finished then the end will come. There will be no more life to give to feed the brain so the body will start to decay, which is a gradual process until there is no more life left. When there is no more life left the decaying system is no more because there is no more decaying to do and no more life to decay.

As life is no more and there is no more life

to give the sun will rise and dry all remains to a dust so there is no more trace of life in this world. All life whether in sea, air or earth will be no more, with no trace of life anywhere in the world we live. The world will go back to dust. A vast shaking of the world will wipe any memory of life from the world. Everything that was made will go back to dust. All life will become dust. There will be no more trace.

Chapter 9

UNDERSTANDING HEAVENLY KNOWLEDGE

The purpose of me writing this book is so that knowledge and understanding, which is heavenly knowledge and understanding can be understood by us as fleshly beings. I am writing this book so we can understand the purpose of life on the earth in a heavenly way.

God has left in this world a knowledge and understanding that we can gather in a vessel in our brain, which is heavenly, so our mind, which is heavenly can go to the vessel filled with heavenly knowledge. This gives us an understanding of what is to come and where we go and our purpose in this world. We have a mind that is heavenly going to a vessel that is heavenly feeding the brain with heavenly knowledge so we can have comfort in knowing our purpose. This is so that as the end of life in this world comes we can have a peaceful mind and know our ending and our purpose.

When heavenly knowledge first came into this world some of the heavenly knowledge was to comfort all beings at the end of time. This was so that this knowledge would guide them to knowing their purpose in life and give them understanding of heavenly things. This knowledge would comfort any being that fills the heavenly vessel that is in every being so that any being having this knowledge in its heavenly vessel will know the purpose and ending of life in this world. This enables us to be guided with a heavenly knowledge and be adopted with this knowledge guiding our brain to being a heavenly being.

As we are heavenly beings in that we are fed with heavenly knowledge, knowledge guides you to knowing you are a son, brother and saint. You are a son because the heavenly mind feeding the brain adopts you to be a son and brother to all who are guided with this knowledge. You are a saint because you are guided with heavenly knowledge making you a saint, not in the eyes of the flesh, but in the eyes of God. His knowledge you have in you makes you so.

As promised in the beginning when God's knowledge came into this world, in the end times the comforter will come. We will be comforted in the end times by knowledge, which is meant for this time. This is now here because the end times are here and as promised the coming of knowledge to comfort us is here.

We as beings whether male or female, will be comforted. Male and female who have this knowledge and are guided to know heavenly things will become heavenly beings through the knowledge that has come, making male and female one understanding knowing both are sons, brothers and saints because the knowledge tells us so.

When we get this heavenly knowledge to fill the vessel that is heavenly we will have two knowledges separated, one knowledge which is fleshly guiding us to a fleshly character in a fleshly vessel and a mind that is fleshly filling the brain to being a fleshly character. We will have one vessel filled with heavenly knowledge and a heavenly mind filling the brain with heavenly knowledge making a heavenly character. These are two minds and two vessels filled with different knowledge, one heavenly and one fleshly.

When we are in a private place and drawing on knowledge, which is heavenly, we are guided to know heavenly things at that time. We are guided by knowledge to knowing we are a heavenly being because our brain is only filled with heavenly knowledge. This knowledge tells us whether male or female that we are sons, brothers and saints not in the eyes of the flesh but in the eyes of God. It is heavenly knowledge we have guiding us. This heavenly being we are is only a heavenly being while in that heavenly state of mind. When heavenly knowledge goes back to the heavenly vessel the fleshly mind fills the brain with fleshly knowledge and goes back to being the character of the flesh that we are, male or female, this is because it is the knowledge in the brain that makes you the character you are. Characters in this world guided by fleshly knowledge are characters of a fleshly being whether male or female. A fleshly mind trying to understand heavenly knowledge makes the character a confused character. Fleshly knowledge in a fleshly vessel in the mind, which is fleshly, drawing knowledge from that vessel which is fleshly, becomes confused. The characters being guided by this confused knowledge become confused themselves.

Knowledge from a heavenly place is in this world to give understanding in a heavenly way so there is no more confusion by separating the fleshly knowledge from the heavenly knowledge. We as fleshly beings drawing fleshly knowledge with a fleshly mind to feed the brain guiding us to know fleshly things can now have our heavenly vessel filled with heavenly knowledge. The mind we have which is heavenly can draw heavenly knowledge from the heavenly vessel that is filled with heavenly knowledge. Our brain can be guided by heavenly knowledge to understanding heavenly things.

Our purpose and our destination and the end times are told to us by this heavenly knowledge which we as beings nearing the end of our lives in this world are now able to receive to comfort us so we will know the truth of our purpose and destination. This knowledge is only here for the end times so we can be comforted by this heavenly knowledge.

God promised he would come in the end times and he has kept his promise by putting this knowledge in this world, so he would come to us in the end, not in person but in knowledge. We are unique in that we have a brain that can be guided with fleshly knowledge and heavenly knowledge from two separate vessels with two minds. In the end times the fleshly character we were before the end times, before the end comes, we as beings nearing the end times can be two characters, one fleshly character and one heavenly character. This is so that the unique brain we have in the last times can walk as a fleshly character while we are still alive and a heavenly character while we are still alive. We can be a fleshly character and a heavenly character in one body.

We in the last time can experience a heavenly mind giving us a peaceful state of mind in knowing that we as beings in the last times can experience being a heavenly being because of the heavenly knowledge feeding the brain in a private place. This tells you as a being in the last times you are a son, because the knowledge, which is heavenly makes you a son. This knowledge, which is heavenly, makes you a brother to all beings that have this knowledge guiding them. You are a saint because the heavenly knowledge makes you a saint not in the eyes of the flesh, but in the eyes of God. It is God's knowledge that tells you so. Our brain was made for this purpose to guide us from the beginning to the end so we in the end can be comforted knowing these things through heavenly knowledge telling us so.

Because our purpose in this world is coming to an end and we are not needed anymore the knowledge, which is heavenly has come to tell us so, so we will understand our purpose and why life in this world has to end this way. Because life in this world was only made temporary, there is a beginning and also an ending. Heavenly knowledge for the end gives you an understanding that takes you from being a fleshly being knowing fleshly things to a heavenly being knowing heavenly things. A likeness of the heavenly being is shown to you in that when God created the being, which was in this world to show heavenly things representing him, he would show him in the likeness of a heavenly being. This was so in the end of time this knowledge can be received to all beings that have this vessel which is opened up so the heavenly knowledge can fill this vessel to guide you as a being to a heavenly state of mind making you a heavenly being. You will have a likeness as a fleshly being and a likeness as a heavenly being in that God shows you through his being he made to represent him a likeness as a fleshly being and a likeness as a heavenly being. In the end times we beings can be a fleshly being with a fleshly likeness and a heavenly being with a heavenly likeness.

When we walk in this world in a fleshly likeness, we can also walk in this world in a heavenly likeness. The likeness of the heavenly being is seen by the being that this heavenly knowledge is in and he who has this knowledge will recognise other beings walking in the world who have this heavenly knowledge. They see themselves as a likeness of a heavenly being so you will see them as a heavenly being. They will recognise you as a heavenly being because of the same likeness and knowledge, which makes you one. A heavenly being likeness and one heavenly knowledge making you all one. Fleshly beings with a fleshly mind not knowing the heavenly mind will not recognise a fleshly being guided by heavenly knowledge because he only sees a fleshly being. A fleshly being that is guided by heavenly knowledge will recognise a fleshly being with heavenly knowledge making them one with God. All fleshly beings with this knowledge and likeness will be one with God because the knowledge tells you so.

This knowledge and likeness can only be achieved in the end times to comfort us from the things to come. Now as God promised his knowledge and likeness is here so we can be at peace knowing a peaceful knowledge and knowing we are a heavenly being and likeness making us a peaceful heavenly being.

Beings that are here at the end are judged accordingly as I have written in this book on the process of dying at the end, beings who die before the end of time do not go anywhere and are only remembered and judged by people who knew them. Thoughts and whispers about them are not needed because they talk between themselves, whether good or bad things about the person who died. Whether they say good or bad about you or remember you in a good or bad way you live in their minds. You are judged when you are dead by people's thoughts about you while they are still alive. People who die before the last days have their character judged by living people, by people who live with them and know them.

When a body dies it is not for God to judge that life but people who knew that life. Thoughts and whispers about you are received in the end because there is no one alive to judge you so it is the thoughts and whispers in the end time that judge you, whether you are judged as a fleshly being in the life you have led which people close to you or know you have thoughts and whispers about you while you are alive, or whether you are judged as a heavenly being at the end by the knowledge you have received which will fill the brain in the last times. If you were a heavenly being before you die so the thoughts of heavenly things will be in that mind before you die giving that heavenly peaceful understanding comforting you at the end of your life. The character who has no heavenly knowledge in their heavenly vessel will receive fleshly thoughts and whispers in the way that they have lived their life from beings that have lived with them or know them and it is their thoughts and whispers that will judge them in the end times.

God will not judge you in the end times because he does not know you. Only people who know or see you will have thoughts and whispers about you. The thoughts and whispers you will have of other people you know or see will go to the people that you aim those thoughts and whispers at.

This knowledge which is heavenly and is only here for beings in the world in the end times is here to comfort all beings of the world at their time of need which will be in the end times. This heavenly knowledge is here now for that purpose.

If you as a being in this world need to know heavenly things unlock the vessel, which is heavenly in your brain so the heavenly knowledge can come into that vessel to guide you to an understanding of the purpose of you being in this world. The brain in the beginning and the fleshly vessel was filled with little knowledge to guide it. Now the brain in the end times as a vessel is filled nearly to capacity with fleshly knowledge guiding us to a fleshly character and a fleshly understanding. In the end times our brain which is unique can now create two characters, one fleshly and one heavenly and can now fulfil and complete its purpose which can only be filled in the end times. Because our vessel is nearly filled with fleshly things our heavenly vessel can now be opened to receive heavenly knowledge in the end times. This knowledge is only here at the end times to bring a oneness in the world of one knowledge which is heavenly in all beings male or female. One understanding creating one heavenly being and one likeness, so that we as beings in the last times have a vessel, which was shut but is now open. If we as beings want this knowledge in the last times, this vessel which was shut can now be opened so we can have a heavenly knowledge filling this heavenly vessel so the mind which is heavenly can take over from the mind which is fleshly and draw knowledge from that vessel filled with heavenly knowledge. This guides the brain to knowing whether male or female that we have a heavenly likeness and are heavenly beings. So we can walk in this world in the last time as a fleshly being and a heavenly being as the example that God made in this world to show us the being that we can be in the last time, whether male or female.

So when we have this heavenly knowledge we could be one with God knowing that we are heavenly beings by the knowledge telling us so. The fleshly character recognises fleshly characters and the heavenly character within recognises heavenly characters. If a fleshly character male or female meets another male or female with a heavenly being inside, the fleshly character will greet the fleshly character and the heavenly character will greet the heavenly character both recognising their own selves and their own kind.

This will bring peace in the world and a

oneness in that there will be one knowledge which is heavenly and one likeness which is heavenly. Peace will be brought to the world in the end times by this oneness. By putting on this oneness and walking the world with this oneness while we are still alive will give you who have this knowledge a peaceful mind and understanding and purpose. We in the end times can have peace with ourselves because this knowledge has healed the confused fleshly mind so we can walk in this world with a mind that is at peace and a oneness.

As promised God's knowledge and understanding has come to save us in the end times. It is not here to judge us it is here to save us by giving you peace and understanding to a oneness. This makes you at one with him in his knowledge that he has given to us in the end times so we will not be confused in trying to understand heavenly things with a fleshly mind, because now we have a mind, which is heavenly telling us heavenly things. The confused mind will be healed to be in a peaceful mind only having to understand fleshly things, if we as beings carry on being fleshly beings with a fleshly mind and are happy in our way of life as a fleshly being, this knowledge is not here to judge but to heal the confused mind. Therefore you live your lives accordingly whether you live your life trying to understand heavenly things with your fleshly mind or whether you live your life understanding heavenly things with a heavenly mind. You will not be judged on which way you choose. It is up to each individual male or female in what they decide to do.

God will not judge you on which way you choose to live your life in the end times.

Chapter 10

A ONENESS IN ALL

All through the ages, since the creation of two beings made by God to represent a heavenly way of life in which they had a choice in how they would make this way of life and they chose the fleshly way in making this life, we as beings from that time have only had one vessel open which is fleshly and one fleshly mind guiding us to heavenly things. This is because God shut the heavenly vessel and the heavenly mind up because only one mind and vessel was needed. Gods heavenly knowledge that he put in the world to guide us to heavenly things was only read and understood by a fleshly mind.

God had his knowledge in this world in books written by beings whom he chose to write his heavenly knowledge, with the mind that he opened up in the people he chose which was the heavenly mind. His heavenly knowledge was written in books so that when the heavenly vessel was shut, knowledge which was heavenly was in books written by the heavenly mind of these beings that he chose. All heavenly knowledge in this world is in books, so God and his knowledge is stored in books and we through the ages read these books with a fleshly mind and get a fleshly understanding of heavenly things.

Now as God promised in the end times we will have an understanding of heavenly things in a heavenly way. Our heavenly mind that we now can open and our vessel which is heavenly, can now be filled with heavenly knowledge, so that we as beings can now be guided by a mind which is heavenly that gathers knowledge from our heavenly vessel now being filled with heavenly knowledge.

We in the end times have the choice in whether to understand heavenly things with a fleshly mind or heavenly things with a heavenly mind. Because the fleshly mind now has run its course and is just one mind guiding us, now we have a choice as God promised in the end times. We have a choice of two minds guiding us in knowing fleshly things with a fleshly mind and heavenly things with a heavenly mind and a vessel filled with fleshly things for a fleshly mind and a heavenly vessel filled with heavenly things for a heavenly mind. This heavenly knowledge can only go back to a heavenly vessel, so that the mind that is heavenly can feed heavenly knowledge from this heavenly vessel guiding the brain to being and knowing that we can be a heavenly being and have a heavenly likeness. The knowledge, which is heavenly in the heavenly vessel, is there to tell us so and give us understanding of the heavenly being we are.

In the end times we have the choice so that peace is brought to the earth by the oneness of all beings male and female, having a choice in whether they stay just being a fleshly being or opening up the vessel which is heavenly and through this vessel becoming a heavenly being as well as being a fleshly being, because the fleshly being is first and the heavenly being is second. We are a fleshly being in a fleshly world and a heavenly being within the fleshly being we are.

Only a fleshly being that has a heavenly being within will recognise another fleshly being with a heavenly being within. Therefore the fleshly being in a fleshly place is still a fleshly being.

This knowledge that is written in this book is from the vessel which is heavenly that I have had opened in me, so my mind which is heavenly can go to that vessel which is heavenly and feed my brain with heavenly knowledge so that I can write heavenly knowledge from this vessel which is heavenly. So that beings in this world can read the knowledge that I have been guided to write from my heavenly vessel so that they male or female can fill their vessel, which they can now open through the scriptures which are in this world for that purpose in the end times. All beings in the world male or female can receive this heavenly knowledge in the heavenly vessel they have in the brain because this heavenly knowledge can only fill the heavenly vessel because it is a heavenly vessel and can only receive heavenly knowledge.

You have to open the vessel in your brain, which is heavenly before you can receive this heavenly knowledge. So I as a being which is fleshly have been guided to write this knowledge from my heavenly vessel, to give you understanding in the end times to guide you to knowing that you have a heavenly vessel and a heavenly mind which has been shut until now and that we have been using our fleshly mind and fleshly vessel guiding us to know heavenly things when it only knows fleshly things.

Now in the end times I have been guided to tell you these things because now we have a choice of having a heavenly mind and a heavenly vessel to guide us along side the fleshly mind and the fleshly vessel. So we will know fleshly things for a fleshly mind and know heavenly things for a heavenly mind, the fleshly mind creating a character which is fleshly and a heavenly mind creating a character within the fleshly being which is a heavenly character.

I have been guided to tell you these things for the end times and only in the end times can we understand these things which are heavenly, because as God promised he would comfort us in the end times. So now we have heavenly knowledge that can be received by us to guide us and comfort us in the end times. Now God has come to me and opened my mind which is heavenly and has guided me through the mind that I have had opened which is heavenly, using me to write this heavenly knowledge that he wants us as fleshly beings to understand that he is with us in the end times. It is this heavenly knowledge that he wants us to understand and know to guide us to being a heavenly being with a heavenly likeness so he can make us whether male or female, sons, brothers and saints and a likeness of a son, brother and saint so he knows you as a son, brother and saint that you are now because the heavenly knowledge tells you so.

Our unique brain that we have can be used in the end times to its full capacity, so the brain can be used to create a fleshly character and a heavenly character. One fleshly character with knowledge filling the vessel which is fleshly so the character grows as the knowledge grows into a character which is fleshly and one heavenly being with knowledge filling the vessel which is heavenly so the being grows as the knowledge grows into a being which is heavenly. Only in the end times can the brain be used fully for what it was made for, so the choice we have is that we have knowledge in the world, which is fleshly and knowledge which is heavenly.

We have books written in this world, which are heavenly, the fleshly books written by the fleshly mind and the heavenly books written by the heavenly mind, which God opened in chosen beings. These beings would write his heavenly knowledge to be remembered in books. The books would last throughout the time until this knowledge, which is heavenly would be required. Now it is time for these books with heavenly knowledge in to be read by us as beings so that the knowledge, which is heavenly in these books, can enter the vessel that we all have in our brain that can contain this heavenly knowledge.

This heavenly knowledge can only be contained in a vessel that is heavenly that we have in our brain, so as the knowledge gradually fills the vessel, which is heavenly, it produces a character, which is heavenly. The brain in this end times can produce a character, which is fleshly and a character, which is heavenly.

The fleshly character grows first and the heavenly character grows second. We have a fleshly character and a heavenly character created by the brain so that we have two characters, two understandings and two likenesses, which can be seen by all who have received this heavenly knowledge. We as beings that are fleshly have to decide which books contain heavenly knowledge to guide us to being heavenly beings while we are still fleshly beings, because only heavenly knowledge we have in books can go back to the heavenly vessel that we have to make us grow into heavenly beings. We have to choose the right knowledge to fill that vessel, because only heavenly knowledge from that heavenly vessel can enter into a heavenly vessel to grow into a heavenly being and a heavenly likeness. Therefore if that vessel which is heavenly is open you can distinguish heavenly knowledge from fleshly knowledge, because the heavenly knowledge guides you to an understanding of heavenly things in a heavenly way.

If you listen to beings talking with a fleshly mind about heavenly things you walk by because your mind, which is heavenly will not recognise this knowledge that these beings have spoken because now you will understand only heavenly things in a heavenly way. If the being is talking about heavenly things from this heavenly vessel then you will understand the heavenly things he has spoken now you have ears that recognise heavenly knowledge being spoken, so your vessel which is heavenly can receive a heavenly knowledge that is being spoken. Therefore a heavenly being will recognise heavenly knowledge from a heavenly being speaking words of heavenly things, with your ears recognising heavenly things and your eyes reading heavenly things and your mouth speaking heavenly things. Your character now, which is heavenly, has a likeness of a heavenly being, so now you are using the facilities you have in hearing, seeing and speaking for heavenly things. Now the character that is created which is heavenly can now speak, see and hear by using these facilities, which the body provides, so you have through the body a physical way of hearing, seeing and speaking heavenly things from the vessel which is heavenly.

When you are in that private place filling that vessel with heavenly knowledge from books you are reading which are heavenly which contain heavenly knowledge, the knowledge guides you from within to hearing and seeing and speaking, so you have the knowledge within speaking, seeing and hearing in a heavenly way and not a fleshly way.

So when we walk in this world we are two

characters knowing fleshly things with a fleshly mind guiding us and we also know heavenly things with a heavenly mind guiding us. So we have two characters in one body each knowing their own kind because they each have their own knowledge guiding them and they each have their own likeness. The fleshly likeness is on the outside and the heavenly likeness is within, each knowing their own likeness.

Now God has a heavenly being within you so he knows you and you know him through this heavenly being that you have in you. So you are one with God because he has made you so with this knowledge and likeness that he has shown us. So now in the last times with this knowledge and our vessel, which is heavenly that we have opened up we can be one with God and at peace knowing, we are all one in likeness with one knowledge telling us so.

Chapter 11

WHY WE ALL NEED THE COMFORTER

Why the comforter has come is to fill the vessel that is heavenly with heavenly knowledge, so when the thoughts and whispers about you as a fleshly character that you were, come to you in the end times they cannot enter into this vessel because the vessel has a heavenly being within that this knowledge which is heavenly has grown in this vessel.

When the thoughts and whispers see that there is a heavenly being within this vessel it cannot enter in so it goes looking for the fleshly character it has come to see in other vessels that are empty. So if your vessel is empty, not only will you have thoughts and whispers judging you in this world of the way you have been in this world, you will also have thoughts and whispers entering in of other fleshly characters who have lived in this world. So you will have thoughts and whispers of your own fleshly character and other fleshly characters too, because the thoughts and whispers can only enter empty heavenly vessels. So if your heavenly vessel is full of heavenly knowledge the thoughts and whispers cannot enter in.

The thoughts and whispers are made to judge characters they have lived with, known or seen and how they see you as a character in this world. They come to judge you and how you have lived and presented yourself in this world, as you yourself have judged others with your thoughts and whispers who you have lived with, known and seen living in this world. You judge people how they have lived and they judge you how you have lived and presented yourself. All thoughts and whispers are here to judge at the end of life in this world.

That is why God promised a comforter in the end of life in this world to protect any character that is still living in this world in the end times, by having this vessel opened which is heavenly and filled with heavenly knowledge which will grow into a heavenly being with a likeness of a heavenly being. As life ends in this world the vessels will open up, one releasing thoughts and whispers of other characters in this world you have known, seen or lived with and the vessel which is heavenly opening up but not allowing any thoughts and whispers that come to you at the end of your life come in to judge you.

The filling of this heavenly vessel for the end of your life is essential if you do not want to be judged by the thoughts and whispers, which will come at the end of life in this world.

As God promised the comforter is here to protect you from the judgement of thoughts and whispers in the end times.